Alex Slate

The New Normal, New Leadership

Leading successfully in the working world of today and tomorrow

Contents

Foreword 8

Disclaimer 10

Chapter 1 The new era of work 11

    Introduction: A turning point in the world of work 11

    1)   The new role of the manager 12

    2)   Diversity and purpose: drivers of the new world of work 14

    3)   Agile methods: A helpful approach, but not the only solution 16

    4)   Extreme ownership: responsibility as a cornerstone 18

    5)   Practical approaches for managers 19

    6)   Conclusion: Leadership in the new world of work 20

Chapter 2 Remote Work - Management from a distance 21

    Introduction: The new reality of remote working 21

    1)   The key principles of remote leadership 22

    2)   Purpose in remote work: Connecting meaning despite distance 25

    3)   Challenges of remote leadership and solutions 26

    4)   Extreme ownership in the remote setup 28

    5)   Technological tools for remote teams 29

    6)   Practical example: My team in remote setup 30

    7)   Conclusion: Remote leadership as a core competence of the future 31

Chapter 3 Back to the office - challenges and opportunities 32

Introduction: The return to a changed world of work 32
1) The new role of the office 33
2) The perspectives of the generations 35
3) Purpose as a motivator for the return 37
4) The challenges of returning and how to overcome them 38
5) Agile methods to support the return 40
6) Extreme ownership: taking responsibility for the return 41
7) Practical example: My team back in the office 42
8) Conclusion: The return as an opportunity 43

Chapter 4 Hybrid working models - finding the balance 44
Introduction: The future of work is hybrid 44
1) The advantages and challenges of hybrid models 45
2) Cultural foundations for hybrid teams 46
3) Generational perspectives on hybrid models 47
4) Practical approaches for the introduction of hybrid models ..49
5) Making purpose visible in hybrid models 51
6) Extreme ownership in hybrid teams 52
7) Practical example: My team and hybrid models 53
8) Conclusion: Finding the balance 54

Chapter 5 Recognizing emotional intelligence and purpose 55
Introduction: Leadership needs more than specialist knowledge ...55
1) The four pillars of emotional intelligence for managers 56
2) Purpose: A key motivator - but not the same for everyone ...58

- 3) Generations and their view of purpose 60
- 4) Emotional intelligence in a hybrid context 62
- 5) Extreme ownership: Emotional intelligence and responsibility 63
- 6) Practical example: Emotional intelligence and purpose in my team 64
- 7) Conclusion: Emotional intelligence and purpose as leadership tools 65

Chapter 6 Leading with clarity and vision 66

Introduction: Leadership without vision is like sailing without a compass 66

- 1) Why visions are so important 67
- 2) The role of clarity in leadership 69
- 3) Vision and clarity for different roles and generations 71
- 4) Practical approaches to developing and implementing a vision 73
- 5) Purpose and vision: two sides of the same coin 74
- 6) Extreme ownership: vision and responsibility 75
- 7) Practical example: Vision and clarity in my team 76
- 8) Conclusion: Clarity and vision as a leadership compass 78

Chapter 7 Discipline and freedom - the leadership mindset 79

Introduction: Freedom comes from structure 79

- 1) Discipline as the basis for successful teams 80
- 2) Freedom through discipline 81

3)	The leadership mindset: balancing discipline and freedom	...82
4)	Discipline and freedom in hybrid teams	...84
5)	Promoting purpose through discipline and freedom	...85
6)	Extreme ownership: discipline and freedom in practice	...86
7)	Practical example: Discipline and freedom in my team	...87
8)	Conclusion: Discipline and freedom as success factors	...88

Chapter 8 Purpose as a driver in multigenerational teams ...89

Introduction: Purpose as a common foundation ...89

1)	Why purpose is crucial	...90
2)	Purpose and the perspectives of the generations	...91
3)	Purpose in various occupational groups	...93
4)	Purpose as a bridge between generations	...95
5)	Purpose in hybrid teams	...96
6)	Extreme ownership: taking responsibility for purpose	...97
7)	Practical example: Purpose in my team	...98
8)	Conclusion: Purpose as a unifying element	...99
9)	When purpose clashes: leadership with different values	...100
10)	Practical example: Strengthening purpose despite differences	...103
11)	Conclusion: Using differences in values as an opportunity 105	

Chapter 9 Practical examples and lessons learned ...106

Introduction: Learning through experience ...106

- 1) Practical examples: Successful leadership in the modern working world 107
- 2) Lessons learned: Important findings for modern leadership 111
- 3) Conclusion: Practice as the key to developing modern leadership 116

Chapter 10 Looking to the future 117
- Introduction: Leadership in a changing world 117
- 1) Technological developments and their impact on leadership 118
- 2) Generational change and new expectations 120
- 3) Sustainability and social responsibility as management topics 122
- 4) Agility as the key to future viability 124
- 5) Extreme ownership in the working world of tomorrow 126
- 6) Practical example: Future-oriented leadership in my team .. 127
- 7) Conclusion: Leadership with a view to the future 128

Acknowledgments 129

Bibliography 131
- 1) Primary literature 131
- 2) Secondary literature 131
- 3) Online sources 132

Foreword

The world of work has changed fundamentally in recent years. Technological innovations, social upheavals and new working models such as remote work and hybrid approaches have turned our way of working and leading upside down. Managers are faced with the challenge of not only managing efficiently, but also inspiring, motivating and leading their teams through uncertain times.

In my more than eight years as a team leader, I have experienced these changes first-hand. The transition from office to home office and finally to hybrid models was a challenging but also incredibly instructive journey for my team and me. In the process, I realized that modern leadership requires far more than specialist knowledge. Responsibility, clear communication, a strong purpose and the ability to adapt to constantly changing conditions have become essential.

This book is the result of my experiences, observations and findings. It is an invitation to managers to reflect on and further develop their role in the new world of work. The principles and practical examples presented are intended to inspire, support and encourage people to break new ground - not only for the success of the team, but also for personal growth.

I thank you for picking up this book and hope that it provides you with valuable inspiration for your own leadership journey.

Disclaimer

This book has been written with the utmost care and to the best of our knowledge and belief. The contents are for informational and inspirational purposes only and are intended to provide managers with ideas for their professional practice.

The author accepts no liability for the topicality, accuracy and completeness of the information provided. The methods, examples and approaches described are based on personal experience and general principles of leadership. They cannot be applied to all companies, teams or specific situations without adaptation.

The implementation of the contents described in this book is at your own risk. The author is not liable for any damages or losses arising directly or indirectly from the use of the information in this book.

For individual challenges or specific legal, tax or economic issues, it is recommended to consult an expert or advisor.

Chapter 1 The new era of work

Introduction: A turning point in the world of work

The world of work has undergone profound changes in recent years. Technological innovations, globalization and the effects of the COVID-19 pandemic have permanently changed working models and management styles. Remote work, hybrid working models and flexible working hours have become integral parts of modern organizations.

For managers, this change means that traditional methods such as control and rigid hierarchies are no longer sufficient. Today's working world demands flexibility, trust and a management style that responds to the individual needs of employees. Managers need to use a wide range of tools - from clear expectation management and emotional intelligence to structured approaches such as agile methods - to lead teams through these changes.

1) The new role of the manager

The demands placed on managers have changed fundamentally. In the past, they were often seen as central decision-makers and controllers. Today, they take on more diverse roles in order to meet the complex demands of the modern working world:

- **Visionaries:**
  They give their team a clear direction and inspire with a long-term vision that goes beyond individual tasks.

- **Problem solvers:**
  They create the framework conditions so that the team can overcome obstacles independently and only intervene when necessary.

- **Purpose amplifiers:**
  They help their employees to recognize the purpose of their work and link it to the company's goals.

- **Bridge builders:**
  They promote collaboration between different generations, cultural backgrounds and working models. In hybrid teams, they create connections between remote and office employees and ensure a common understanding.

- **Structure providers:**
  They use structured approaches such as agile methods to promote flexibility without allowing chaos.

2) Diversity and purpose: drivers of the new world of work

Diversity within teams is a crucial aspect of the modern working world. Different generations work side by side, each with their own values, working methods and expectations:

- **Baby boomers (before 1965):**
  They value stability, clear structures and personal relationships. For them, purpose often means making a valuable contribution with their experience and knowledge.

- **Generation X (1965-1980):**
  This pragmatic generation values personal responsibility and effective processes. They often see purpose in the balance between professional success and personal well-being.

- **Millennials (1981-1996):**
  Millennials are looking for meaning in their work and attach great importance to flexibility, personal development and a positive corporate culture.

- **Generation Z (from 1997):**
  The youngest generation expects fast results, digital excellence and social responsibility. For them, purpose often means being part of something innovative or sustainable.

Purpose as the key to motivation:

While purpose is often central in creative or people-centered professions (e.g. HR or marketing), in technical professions the focus is often on solving specific problems. Managers must recognize that purpose means something different for each group and respond accordingly.

3) Agile methods: a helpful approach, but not the only solution

Agile principles have their origins in software development, but also offer tools in other areas to guide teams through dynamic environments. They are not the solution to every problem, but they can help to create structure in complex situations.

Agile principles in leadership:

- **Transparency:**
  Regular updates or meetings such as dailies create visibility of progress within the team.

- **Feedback culture:**
  Retrospectives or similar approaches promote open feedback and enable continuous improvement.

- **Iterative processes:**
  Short work cycles (e.g. sprints) offer the opportunity to react flexibly to changes.

Agile methods as a tool, not a panacea:

In your team, approaches such as dailies and retrospectives have helped to strengthen collaboration during the transition to working from home. Agile principles complement other leadership approaches by combining structure and flexibility, but should not dominate alone.

4) Extreme ownership: responsibility as a cornerstone

As Jocko Willink emphasizes in *Extreme Ownership*, responsibility is a central component of modern leadership. Regardless of the methods used, it remains the task of the manager to take responsibility for the success or failure of the team.

Responsibility in practice:

- **Set clear goals:**
  Employees need a clear idea of what is expected of them.

- **Make responsibilities transparent:**
  Clear roles and tasks enable teams to work more effectively.

- **Create trust:**
  By taking responsibility and being a role model, managers promote trust within the team.

5) Practical approaches for managers

- **Promote communication:**
  Regular meetings or one-to-one discussions ensure clarity and build trust.

- **Enable flexibility:**
  Different working models (office, home office, hybrid) should be adapted to the needs of the team.

- **Use methods flexibly:**
  Whether classic leadership, agile methods or a mix of both - the choice of method should suit the situation and the team.

6) Conclusion: Leadership in the new world of work

The new era of work demands more from managers than just specialist knowledge. They must act as visionaries, problem solvers and bridge builders, make purpose visible and use agile methods as supporting tools. A flexible and situational approach that respects the individual needs of team members and strengthens the team as a whole is crucial.

Chapter 2 Remote work - management from a distance

Introduction: The new reality of remote working

Remote work is no longer just a trend, but an established reality in the modern working world. For many companies, the switch to working from home began as a short-term emergency solution, but quickly developed into an established model. Studies show that employees benefit from the flexibility and efficiency of remote working - but this change brings new challenges for managers.

How do you lead a team that doesn't meet in the office every day? How do you create trust when there are no spontaneous conversations at the coffee machine? And how do you motivate employees who work from home? These questions are crucial for the success of remote teams.

1) The key principles of remote leadership

1. trust as a basis

In a remote working environment, trust is the most important pillar for success. Managers need to trust that their employees are doing their jobs responsibly - without the ability to physically monitor them.

Practical tips for trust in the remote team:
- **Set clear expectations:** Agree specific goals and deadlines so that everyone knows what they are being measured against.
- **Encourage open communication:** Create channels for regular updates and feedback.
- **Let go of control:** Instead of micromanaging, focus on results.

2. create structure through agile approaches

Agile methods can help to coordinate remote teams efficiently. Elements such as **daily stand-ups** and **retrospectives** provide orientation and promote team cohesion, even from a distance.

Application in remote work:
- **Dailies:** Short, daily meetings (10-15 minutes) in which each team member shares their current tasks and challenges.

- **Retrospectives:** Regular feedback rounds to reflect on processes and implement improvements.//
- **Kanban boards:** Tools such as Trello or Jira visualize tasks and progress and create transparency.

3. promote personal responsibility

Remote work offers employees more freedom, but also requires more self-discipline. Managers should encourage their teams to take responsibility for their work.

Strategies to promote personal responsibility:

- **Give autonomy:** Let employees plan their own working hours and priorities where possible.
- **Delegate decision-making authority:** Assign responsibility for projects or subtasks to team members.
- **Praise and recognition:** Celebrate successes to reinforce positive behavior.

2) Purpose in remote work: Connecting meaning despite distance

In a remote environment, it is particularly important that employees understand why their work is relevant. Purpose gives employees a sense of belonging and motivates them to give their best even without the physical presence of the team.

The purpose in different occupational groups:

- **Technical teams:**
  Show how their work contributes to larger projects, e.g. through measurable results or the success of a product.

- **Creative roles:**
  Emphasize the emotional impact of their work, e.g. on customers or the corporate culture.

- **HR and C-level roles:**
  Communicate how their decisions shape the long-term direction of the company.

3) Challenges of remote leadership and solutions

1. lack of social interaction

Employees can feel isolated if they cannot have spontaneous conversations with colleagues.

Solution:
- Organize regular virtual team events, such as coffee breaks or game nights.
- Promote peer-to-peer communication through buddy systems or joint projects.

2. communication problems

Misunderstandings arise more easily when communication is mainly in writing.

Solution:
- Use video conferencing for important meetings to incorporate non-verbal signals.
- Establish clear rules for communication, e.g. response times to emails or the use of certain tools.

3. overwork and burnout

Without a clear separation between work and private life, many remote employees tend to work longer hours.

Solution:
- Encourage your team to keep fixed working hours.
- Set an example by drawing clear boundaries between work and leisure.

4) Extreme ownership in the remote setup

As Jocko Willink emphasizes in *Extreme Ownership*, responsibility is the key to successful leadership. In the remote setup, this means:

- **Take responsibility for communication:**
  Managers must ensure that information is shared clearly and in a timely manner.

- **Proactively remove obstacles:**
  Identify challenges faced by your team members at an early stage and support them in finding solutions.

- **Evaluate results instead of processes:**
  Focus on what your team achieves, not on how it works.

5) Technological tools for remote teams

The right tools can make the transition to remote setup much easier. Here are some tried and tested solutions:

- **Communication:** Slack, Microsoft Teams, Zoom
- **Project management:** Trello, Asana, Jira, TFS
- **Collaboration:** Google Workspace, Miro

6) Practical example: My team in remote setup

In my team, the introduction of daily stand-ups and retrospectives played a key role in making the transition from the office to working from home a smooth one. The dailies made it possible to keep track of progress and challenges despite physical distance. Retrospectives promoted an open feedback culture, which not only enabled continuous improvements, but also helped to maintain social cohesion within the team.

We mainly used **Microsoft Teams**, **Miro** and **TFS** as tools. These tools supported transparent communication and facilitated coordinated collaboration in a hybrid working environment. This allowed us to remain flexible and respond to the individual needs of the team members.

7) Conclusion: Remote leadership as a core competence of the future

Remote work presents managers with new challenges, but also offers enormous opportunities. By creating trust, making purpose visible and integrating structure through agile approaches, you can lead your team successfully despite physical distance. The ability to master remote leadership is becoming an indispensable skill in the new era of work.

Chapter 3 Back to the office - challenges and opportunities

Introduction: The return to a changed world of work

After months or even years of working from home, many companies are faced with the task of bringing their employees back to the office. However, the return is often more complex than expected. While some employees appreciate the social interaction and routine of office life, others see no added value in returning to the office if they can complete their tasks efficiently from home.

These tensions affect teams differently: older employees may prefer the familiar office environment, while younger generations appreciate the flexibility of remote working. The challenge for managers is to find a balance that meets everyone's needs without losing sight of the company's goals.

1) The new role of the office

The office has changed from a mandatory workplace to a place of collaboration, innovation and cultural development. Managers need to recognize this change and consciously reposition the office:

- **Place of collaboration:**
  Promote teamwork through joint workshops, brainstorming sessions and problem solving, which are more difficult to implement in the home office.

- **Place of innovation:**
  Spaces for creative processes and informal discussions can promote innovation and knowledge exchange.

- **Place of corporate culture:**
  Face-to-face events and rituals strengthen cohesion and identification with the company.

Practical approaches:

- Design flexible offices, e.g. with hot-desking or meeting areas that are suitable for both hybrid and purely physical work.

- Create attractive incentives for returning employees, such as joint events, further training opportunities or targeted team-building activities.

2) The perspectives of the generations

1. **Baby boomers (before 1965):**

   - **Attitude:** This generation often prefers personal interaction in the office and appreciates clear structures.

   - **Challenge:** Ensure that they continue to feel valued in the office and that their experience is made visible.

   - **Approach:** Actively involve them in mentoring activities or knowledge transfer.

2. **Generation X (1965-1980):**

   - **Attitude:** She values personal responsibility and pragmatic solutions, but is prepared to come into the office if the benefits are clearly recognizable.

   - **Challenge:** Avoid unnecessary attendance obligations that could be perceived as inefficient.

   - **Approach:** Communicate clearly when and why physical presence makes sense.

3. **Millennials (1981-1996):**

    - **Attitude:** They prefer flexibility and question the point of returning to the office more than other generations.
    - **Challenge:** Create a purpose that goes beyond mere presence.
    - **Approach:** Emphasize the social and cultural importance of the office, e.g. through networking opportunities.

4. **Generation Z (from 1997):**

    - **Attitude:** This generation is tech-savvy and expects a seamless integration of digital and physical ways of working.
    - **Challenge:** She could quickly feel bored if the office is perceived as inflexible.
    - **Approach:** Integrate innovative technologies and promote an open feedback culture.

3) Purpose as a motivator for the return

A strong purpose can help make returning to the office a meaningful decision. Managers should clearly communicate the value of office work:

- **For technical teams:**
  Show how physical meetings can solve technical problems faster and promote innovation.

- **For creative roles:**
  Emphasize the benefits of face-to-face brainstorming sessions and the opportunity to get direct inspiration from colleagues.

- **For HR and leadership roles:**
  Emphasize the importance of the office in building company culture and fostering interpersonal relationships.

4) The challenges of returning and how to overcome them

1. resistance to the return

Some employees feel more productive working from home and see no need to return to the office.

Solution:
- Make sure that the return is well justified, e.g. by the need for teamwork or specific projects.
- Offer hybrid working models that combine flexibility with presence.

2. loss of social cohesion

After working from home for a long time, some employees may feel alienated.

Solution:
- Organize team-building activities to rebuild relationships.
- Encourage informal meetings, such as coffee breaks or joint lunches.

3. logistical challenges

A lack of space or unclear rules for hybrid models can make it difficult to return to the office.

Solution:
- Implement hot-desking and flexible workstations.
- Communicate clear rules about when and how the office should be used.

5) Agile methods to support the return

Agile principles can help to ease the transition to the office without reintroducing rigid structures.

- **Dailies:**
  Use short meetings to create clarity about the day's goals and to promote exchange.

- **Retrospectives:**
  Regularly analyze what works in hybrid collaboration and where improvements are needed.

- **Sprints:**
  Plan the return in small, iterative steps in order to be able to react flexibly to feedback.

6) Extreme ownership: taking responsibility for the return

The return to the office is a critical moment that places particular demands on the manager. It is their responsibility to make the return a positive experience.

Practical approaches:
- Take feedback from your team seriously and adjust the plans if necessary.
- Communicate clearly and transparently why the return is necessary and what benefits it will bring.
- Be a role model by actively taking advantage of the benefits of office work yourself.

7) Practical example: My team back in the office

In my team, the return to the office was initially met with skepticism. Many had become accustomed to the flexibility of working from home and questioned the added value of mandatory attendance.

Targeted measures made it possible to shape the return in a positive way:

- **Agile approaches:** We used retrospectives to collect feedback and iteratively improve the return process.
- **Flexibility**: Hybrid models allowed team members to continue working from home whenever it made sense.
- **Purpose:** We made sure that every office presence had a clear purpose, e.g. for technical discussions or creative workshops.

The result: social cohesion within the team was strengthened and acceptance of hybrid models increased considerably.

8) Conclusion: The return as an opportunity

The return to the office is not a return to the past, but an opportunity to redefine the office. Leaders who emphasize purpose, consider generational perspectives and apply agile principles flexibly can successfully manage this transition. The office can become a place that fosters collaboration, innovation and culture - a valuable complement to the flexibility of the home office.

Chapter 4 Hybrid working models - finding the balance

Introduction: The future of work is hybrid

Hybrid working models have established themselves as the preferred solution for many companies. They combine the best of both worlds: the flexibility of working from home and the social and creative benefits of office work. However, introducing and managing hybrid models is anything but easy.

Managers are faced with the challenge of creating clear structures, taking into account the individual needs of employees and at the same time ensuring that team dynamics do not suffer. Hybrid working models require more than just technical tools - they demand a new understanding of leadership, communication and collaboration.

1) The advantages and challenges of hybrid models

Advantages:
1. **Flexibility:**
   Employees can adapt their place of work to their tasks and personal needs.

2. **Satisfaction and productivity:**
   Studies show that hybrid working improves the work-life balance and increases motivation.

3. **Cost reduction:**
   Companies can save costs by reducing office space.

Challenges:
1. **Inequality between remote and office employees:**
   There is a risk that employees in the office are given preferential treatment.

2. **Communication:**
   Without clear rules, collaboration between remote and office teams can suffer.

3. **Technology:**
   Technical barriers or inadequate tools can impair efficiency.

2) Cultural foundations for hybrid teams

The basis for hybrid working models is a strong corporate culture based on trust, openness and collaboration.

Core principles:
1. **Equal rights:**
   All team members, whether on-site or remote, should have the same opportunities to participate.

2. **Transparency:**
   Information must be easily accessible to everyone, regardless of where they work.

3. **Flexibility:**
   Managers should give employees the freedom to design hybrid models individually.

3) Generational perspectives on hybrid models

1. **Baby boomers (before 1965):**

   - **Attitude:** Often prefer to work in the office because they value personal interaction and clear structures.

   - **Challenge:** You might feel isolated working from home.

   - **Approach:** Offer them regular office hours and the opportunity to pass on knowledge to younger colleagues.

2. **2nd Generation X (1965-1980):**

   - **Attitude:** values pragmatic solutions and efficiency, is open to hybrid approaches.

   - **Challenge:** You may find hybrid models inefficient if the structure is unclear.

   - **Approach:** Communicate clear rules and support them with effective tools.

3. **Millennials (1981-1996):**

    - **Attitude:** They appreciate the flexibility of hybrid models and want to decide for themselves when they come into the office.

    - **Challenge:** You might feel put off by fixed office hours.

    - **Approach:** Offer maximum flexibility and emphasize the importance of attendance times.

4. **Generation Z (from 1997):**

    - **Attitude:** This tech-savvy generation expects a seamless integration of digital and physical work.

    - **Challenge:** She may find hybrid models superfluous if remote options work well.

    - **Approach:** Use innovative technologies and encourage regular face-to-face meetings for social cohesion.

4) Practical approaches for the introduction of hybrid models

1. **Create clear rules and expectations**

   - Define when and why employees should come to the office (e.g. for team meetings or creative workshops).
   - Communicate expectations openly and transparently to avoid misunderstandings.

2. **Ensuring technological support**

   - Invest in tools that facilitate hybrid collaboration, e.g. Microsoft Teams, Miro or TFS.
   - Create seamless integration between remote and office workplaces through hybrid meeting rooms or collaboration tools.

3. **Promote social interaction**

   - Organize regular team events, both online and on site.
   - Use informal activities to strengthen social cohesion.

4. **Integrating agility into hybrid teams**

    - **Dailies:** Hold short meetings to promote exchange between remote and office employees.

    - **Retrospectives:** Regularly analyze how the hybrid model works and adapt it.

    - **Sprints:** Plan work cycles that are suitable for both remote and office work.

5) Making purpose visible in hybrid models

A hybrid model can lead to the meaning of work becoming less tangible for some employees. Managers should consciously emphasize purpose:

1. **Technical teams:**
   Show how their work contributes to concrete results regardless of where they work.

2. **Creative roles:**
   Emphasize how collaboration - whether in the office or remotely - enhances creative processes.

3. **HR and managers:**
   Clarify the role of the hybrid model in developing an inclusive corporate culture.

6) Extreme ownership in hybrid teams

As described in *Extreme Ownership*, responsibility is the key to successful leadership. In hybrid teams, this means:

- **Take responsibility for communication:** Ensure that information reaches all team members.

- **Remove obstacles:** Identify and solve problems arising from hybrid working models.

- **Prioritize results:** Focus on what the team achieves, not how or where it works.

7) Practical example: My team and hybrid models

In my team, we have successfully introduced hybrid working models by combining clear structures and agile approaches:

- **Flexibility:** We have defined that office hours can be used for collaborative work such as workshops or technical discussions, while concentrated tasks can be completed in the home office.

- **Agile practices:** Through dailies and retrospectives, we have ensured that all team members are involved, no matter where they work.

- **Social interaction:** Regular team events and hybrid meetings helped to maintain cohesion within the team.

The hybrid model made it possible to take the individual needs of employees into account without jeopardizing team goals.

8) Conclusion: finding the balance

Hybrid working models are not a simple solution, but a challenge that requires careful planning and adaptation. However, leaders who create clear rules, emphasize purpose and integrate agile approaches can develop a model that combines the benefits of office and remote work. The future of work is hybrid - and it offers tremendous opportunities for organizations that are willing to adapt.

Chapter 5 Recognizing emotional intelligence and purpose

Introduction: Leadership needs more than specialist knowledge

Technological innovations and agile methods can solve many challenges, but they cannot replace the core of successful leadership: the interpersonal level. Emotional intelligence - the ability to perceive, understand and respond appropriately to one's own feelings and those of others - is one of the most important skills of a manager today.

Purpose is another decisive factor. Employees who recognize the purpose of their work are more committed, more productive and more satisfied. However, purpose is perceived differently - depending on personality, professional group and generation. Managers need to recognize these differences in order to respond to them individually.

1) The four pillars of emotional intelligence for managers

1. **Self-perception:**

   - Managers need to understand their own emotions and reactions. Only then can they act consciously and not impulsively.

   - **Practice:** Reflect regularly on how you react in certain situations and identify patterns.

2. **Self-regulation:**

   - Controlling emotions does not mean suppressing them, but consciously managing them.

   - **Practice:** Remain calm in stressful situations to give your team a sense of security.

3. **Social perception:**

   - Understand the needs, concerns and motivations of your team.

   - **Practice:** Pay attention to non-verbal signals and make time for regular conversations.

4. **Relationship management:**

    - Cultivate relationships by building trust and resolving conflicts constructively.

    - **Practice:** Use open communication and promote cooperation, even in difficult times.

2) Purpose: A key motivator - but not the same for everyone

Purpose is more than just a buzzword. It gives employees the feeling that they are part of something bigger. But the meaning that people see in their work varies greatly:

1. **Technical professions:**

    - **View of purpose:**
      They appreciate solving tangible problems and seeing results. An abstract purpose ("to change the world") is often less relevant.

    - **Approach:**
      Emphasize the concrete influence of their work, e.g. on the efficiency of a system or the success of a product.

2. **Creative roles (e.g. marketing, design):**

    - **View of purpose:**
    Creative employees are looking for an emotional connection to their work. Purpose often means inspiring people or telling stories.

    - **Approach:**
    Focus on the impact of your work on customers or the brand.

3. **HR and C-level roles:**

    - **View of purpose:**
    You want to shape the corporate culture and exert strategic influence. Purpose means creating long-term value.

    - **Approach:**
    Communicate how their work contributes to the overall strategy and growth of the company.

3) Generations and their view of purpose

1. **Baby boomers (before 1965):**

   - **Expectation:**
   They see purpose in passing on their knowledge and creating stability.

   - **Approach:**
   Recognize their experience and involve them in mentoring activities.

2. **Generation X (1965-1980):**

   - **Expectation:**
   They want to achieve practical and realistic goals that are in line with their values.

   - **Approach:**
   Communicate clear, actionable goals and show how they contribute to the company's success.

3. **Millennials (1981-1996):**

    - **Expectation:**
    They look for meaning in their work and attach great importance to social and ecological responsibility.

    - **Approach:**
    Show how their work has a positive impact on the community or the environment.

4. **Generation Z (from 1997):**

    - **Expectation:**
    You expect purpose as standard and want to have a direct positive impact.

    - **Approach:**
    Offer projects that combine innovation and social responsibility.

4) Emotional intelligence in a hybrid context

Emotional intelligence becomes even more important in hybrid working models, as managers often have less direct contact with their employees.

Challenges:

- **Limited non-verbal communication:** It is more difficult to perceive emotions and moods virtually.
- **Isolation:** Remote employees can feel excluded.

Solutions:

1. **Regular check-ins:**
   Use 1:1 meetings to better understand the individual needs of your employees.

2. **Virtual social activities:**
   Promote social cohesion, e.g. through virtual coffee breaks or hybrid team events.

3. **Feedback culture:**
   Use retrospectives to receive regular feedback and tackle challenges at an early stage.

5) Extreme ownership: emotional intelligence and responsibility

Emotional intelligence requires taking responsibility for one's own emotions and those of the team. Managers should:

- **Admitting your own mistakes:** Authenticity promotes trust.

- **Show empathy:** Put yourself in your employees' shoes to make better decisions.

- **Act proactively:** Recognize problems early and solve them before they escalate.

6) Practical example: Emotional intelligence and purpose in my team

In my team, I have found that purpose depends heavily on the individual roles. While some team members draw their motivation from solving technical challenges, others need a stronger connection to the corporate vision.

Through regular 1:1 meetings, I was able to better understand the different needs. Agile methods such as retrospectives also helped to involve the team as a whole. This made it clear that social cohesion is also important for technical employees - an insight that we integrated into hybrid models.

7) Conclusion: Emotional intelligence and purpose as leadership tools

Managers who actively use emotional intelligence and purpose can better motivate and support their teams. The ability to respond to individual needs while promoting cohesion is crucial in the modern working world. Emotional intelligence and purpose are not opposites, but complementary: they create the basis for successful collaboration in a dynamic and hybrid environment.

Chapter 6 Leading with clarity and vision

Introduction: Leadership without vision is like sailing without a compass

A clear vision is the foundation of successful leadership. It gives teams orientation and motivation, especially in times of change. But vision alone is not enough - it must be clearly communicated and translated into concrete goals.

For managers, this means building a bridge between the overarching corporate strategy and the daily tasks of their teams. This requires clarity, consistency and the ability to adapt the vision to the individual needs and roles of the team members.

1) Why visions are so important

1. provide orientation:

In a dynamic working world in which teams often switch between office, home office and hybrid models, a vision provides structure and direction.

2. create motivation:

An inspiring vision awakens the commitment of employees. They feel part of something bigger that goes beyond their individual tasks.

3. promote unity:

A shared vision creates a common understanding that connects team members despite different work locations or generations.

Practical example:

In my team, we used the vision to create a clear direction and motivation for our work. Our vision was to "actively shape the next generation of a software platform with clear and intuitive interfaces".

This vision served several goals: shorter development times, better collaboration within and between teams, fewer dependencies and the development of more testable software. We used the following approaches to make this vision tangible:

- **Clarity:** We defined measurable milestones, such as the completion of specific modules within a set timeframe, and ensured that everyone in the team clearly understood their roles and responsibilities.

- **Communication:** Regular dailies and retrospectives helped us to review progress, identify challenges at an early stage and continuously integrate the vision into our day-to-day work.

- **Purpose:** We emphasized how our work not only optimizes our internal processes, but also lays the foundation for better collaboration, shorter time-to-market and more sustainable software solutions in the long term.

The result was a team that was more focused on a common goal. This vision not only gave us direction, but also encouraged collaboration and innovation within the team and beyond.

2) The role of clarity in leadership

Clarity is the key to making a vision tangible and achievable. Without clear communication, even the best visions can be misunderstood or ignored.

The importance of responsibility as a leader's core task is impressively described in *Extreme Ownership: How U.S. Navy SEALs Lead and Win* by Jocko Willink and Leif Babin. They emphasize that leaders must always take full responsibility for the success or failure of their team - regardless of external circumstances. This principle, which stems from the experiences of Navy SEALs, can be directly applied to the modern working world: managers should identify and remove obstacles instead of passing on blame. This creates a culture in which teams can work together successfully.

1. formulate goals clearly:
   - **SMART criteria:** Goals should be specific, measurable, achievable, relevant and time-bound.
   - **Example:** Instead of "Let's improve efficiency", the goal could be: "Let's reduce the processing time of projects by 10% within the next three months."

2. regular communication:

A vision must be constantly communicated and linked to daily tasks.

3. create transparency:
   - Explain how individual tasks contribute to achieving the vision.
   - Share progress and recognize successes to keep the team motivated.

3) Vision and clarity for different roles and generations

1. **Technical teams:**

    - **What they need:** Concrete, tangible goals and clear connections between their work and the vision.

    - **Approach:** Show how their work drives innovation or solves problems that are critical to the business.

2. **Creative roles:**

    - **What they need:** Inspiration and freedom to interpret the vision in their own way.

    - **Approach:** Emphasize the emotional and cultural value of their work and encourage them to contribute their own ideas.

3. **Managers and HR:**

    - **What they need:** A strategic vision that integrates long-term values and goals.

    - **Approach:** Communicate how the vision shapes the corporate culture and ensures overall success.

4. **Generations:**

    - **Baby boomers:** value stability and clear goals that incorporate their experience.

    - **Generation X:** Prefer pragmatic approaches and realistic goals.

    - **Millennials:** Looking for meaningful visions that include social or environmental responsibility.

    - **Generation Z:** Expects innovative and future-oriented visions that combine technology and sustainability.

4) Practical approaches to developing and implementing a vision

1. **Developing a vision together:**

   - Involve the team in the process to promote commitment and identification.

   - Use workshops or brainstorming sessions to gather ideas.

2. **Translate vision into concrete steps:**

   - Break down the vision into small, achievable goals that make progress measurable.

   - Use agile approaches such as sprints to achieve goals step by step.

3. **Review and adjust vision regularly:**

   - Reflect with your team on whether the vision is still relevant and whether adjustments need to be made.

   - Use retrospectives to gather feedback and refine the focus.

5) Purpose and vision: two sides of the same coin

Purpose gives employees a sense of purpose, while vision shows the way to get there. Managers must combine both elements in order to lead their teams effectively.

Establish a connection:

- **For technical teams:** Show how the vision translates the purpose into tangible results.

- **For creative roles:** Use the vision to expand the purpose and promote new ideas.

- **For HR and managers:** Use the vision to anchor long-term values and strategies.

6) Extreme ownership: vision and responsibility

As Jocko Willink describes in *Extreme Ownership*, it is up to the manager to clearly formulate the vision and ensure that the team understands and implements it.

Steps towards implementation:
1. **Take responsibility:** Be the first to live the vision and actively implement it.
2. **Remove obstacles:** Help your team overcome challenges that hinder the realization of the vision.
3. **Track results:** Set clear milestones and review progress regularly.

7) Practical example: Vision and clarity in my team

In my team, we used the vision to create a clear direction and motivation for our work. Our vision was to "actively shape the next generation of a software platform with clear and intuitive interfaces".

This vision served several goals: shorter development times, better collaboration within and between teams, fewer dependencies and the development of more testable software. We used the following approaches to make this vision tangible:

- **Clarity:** We defined measurable milestones, such as the completion of specific modules within a set timeframe, and ensured that everyone in the team clearly understood their roles and responsibilities.

- **Communication:** Regular dailies and retrospectives helped us to review progress, identify challenges at an early stage and continuously integrate the vision into our day-to-day work.

- **Purpose:** We emphasized how our work not only optimizes our internal processes, but also lays the foundation for better collaboration, shorter time-to-market and more sustainable software solutions in the long term.

The result was a team that was more focused on a common goal. This vision not only gave us direction, but also encouraged collaboration and innovation within the team and beyond.

8) Conclusion: Clarity and vision as a management compass

A clear vision is essential to inspire and lead teams. But it must be made tangible - through clear communication, measurable goals and a connection to the purpose of the employees. Managers who actively use vision and clarity not only create orientation, but also promote motivation, unity and success.

Chapter 7 Discipline and freedom - the leadership mindset

Introduction: Freedom comes from structure

Many see discipline and freedom as opposites, but in leadership they are closely linked. Discipline creates the foundation on which freedom can flourish. Clear structures, processes and expectations give teams the framework they need to work creatively, flexibly and independently.

A good leadership mindset recognizes when structure is necessary and when it makes sense to leave room for manoeuvre. Finding this balance is particularly crucial in hybrid working models.

1) Discipline as the basis for successful teams

1. **Create clear processes:**

   - Teams need transparent and repeatable processes in order to work efficiently.
   - Example: Define standards for code reviews, communication channels or project documentation.

2. **Promote consistency:**

   - Discipline means sticking to routines, such as regular meetings or updates that provide stability and orientation.
   - Example: Dailies and sprints structure the daily work routine and create reliability.

3. **Establish responsibility:**

   - Discipline promotes a sense of responsibility, as clear procedures and expectations hold individuals accountable.
   - Example: Use tools such as TFS to assign tasks transparently and track their progress.

2) Freedom through discipline

1. **Promote autonomy:**

   - With clear structures in the background, employees can work creatively and independently.

   - Example: In your team, well-documented interfaces made it possible for developers to work independently on modules without having to wait for other teams.

2. **Enable flexibility:**

   - A disciplined foundation makes it possible to react flexibly to new requirements or challenges.

   - Example: Agile methods such as sprints enabled changes in software development to be integrated promptly without jeopardizing overall progress.

3. **Strengthen trust:**

   - Disciplined teams create trust because they act predictably and reliably. This trust gives managers the freedom to let go and hand over control to the team.

3) The leadership mindset: balancing discipline and freedom

A successful manager recognizes when discipline and when freedom is required. This requires:

1. **Situational awareness:**

   - Which tasks require clear guidelines and where can freedom be left?

   - Example: Routine tasks such as tests or reviews need clear processes, while creative tasks such as designing interfaces require freedom.

2. **Adaptability:**

   - Every team member has different needs and ways of working. Adapt your management style accordingly.

   - Example: Experienced developers often need fewer guidelines, while new team members need more structure.

3. Consistency in communication:

- Clear, consistent communication is crucial in order to combine discipline and freedom.

- Example: Communicate which parts of a project can be designed flexibly and which must be strictly adhered to.

4) Discipline and freedom in hybrid teams

1. **Challenges:**

   - Hybrid teams often have different expectations in terms of structure and freedom.
   - Remote employees may feel restricted by too much discipline, while office workers demand more freedom.

2. **Solutions:**

   - **Flexible framework:**
     Establish basic rules for meetings, deadlines and communication that apply to everyone and allow for individual adjustments.

   - **Agile approaches:**
     Use agile methods such as retrospectives to find out what balance of discipline and freedom works best for the team.

   - **Transparent tools:**
     Use tools such as TFS or Miro to make progress visible without micromanaging.

5) Promoting purpose through discipline and freedom

1. **Technical teams:**

   - Clear processes and interfaces make it possible to concentrate on solving problems.
   - Example: Your team was able to work more efficiently thanks to disciplined code standards, which led to shorter development times.

2. **Creative roles:**

   - Freedom is crucial for developing new ideas, but discipline helps to implement them.
   - Example: A well-defined creative process with deadlines and milestones promotes results.

3. **Managers and HR:**

   - Disciplined personnel planning processes create scope for strategic initiatives.
   - Example: A structured feedback culture makes it possible to improve the corporate culture in the long term.

6) Extreme ownership: discipline and freedom in practice

As described in *Extreme Ownership*, it is the manager's responsibility to find the right balance between discipline and freedom.

Practical steps:
1. **Take responsibility:**
   Be the role model for discipline without restricting your team's freedom.

2. **Remove obstacles:**
   Create processes that remove obstacles instead of creating new ones.

3. **Let go of control:**
   Recognize when your team is ready to take responsibility and trust them to make the right decisions.

7) Practical example: Discipline and freedom in my team

In my team, we created a balance between discipline and freedom that increased both the productivity and the satisfaction of the team members:

- **Discipline**: Thanks to clearly defined processes, such as documented interfaces and code standards, we were able to minimize dependencies between the teams. This led to shorter development times and more testable software.

- **Freedom:** Within this framework, the developers had the freedom to find innovative solutions for their modules without being restricted to strict specifications.

- **Agile methods:** Regular dailies and retrospectives helped us to constantly review and adjust the balance.

The result was a team that was able to work efficiently and creatively without losing its bearings.

8) Conclusion: Discipline and freedom as success factors

Discipline and freedom are not opposites, but two sides of the same coin. Managers who successfully combine these elements create an environment in which teams can perform at their best. The foundation is a leadership mindset that promotes both structure and trust and gives employees room to develop.

For readers who want to delve deeper into responsibility as a central principle of leadership, I recommend the book *Extreme Ownership: How U.S. Navy SEALs Lead and Win* by Jocko Willink and Leif Babin. The authors share practical lessons on how to take responsibility in difficult situations and thereby build trust and success - an approach that is also inspiring in the modern working world.

Chapter 8 Purpose as a driver in multigenerational teams

Introduction: Purpose as a common basis

In the modern working world, purpose - the meaning and purpose of a job - is no longer just a bonus, but a key driver of motivation and commitment. However, purpose is not perceived in the same way by everyone. Different generations and professional groups have different expectations and values that shape their understanding of purpose.

The challenge for managers is to create a common purpose that unites everyone without ignoring individual needs.

1) Why purpose is crucial

1. **Increase motivation:**

    - Employees who recognize the meaning of their work are more committed and productive.

2. **Promoting cohesion:**

    - A clearly defined purpose can serve as a common denominator in teams that are otherwise characterized by different backgrounds or working styles.

3. **Retain employees:**

    - Younger generations in particular are looking for meaning in their work and prefer companies that reflect their values.

2) Purpose and the perspectives of the generations

1. **Baby boomers (before 1965):**

   - **What drives them:**
     They find purpose in passing on their knowledge and creating long-term value.

   - **Leadership approach:**
     Offer them opportunities to pass on their experience, e.g. through mentoring programs.

2. **Generation X (1965-1980):**

   - **What drives them:**
     They seek purpose in achieving practical and realistic goals.

   - **Leadership approach:**
     Communicate clear and achievable goals that position their work as part of the bigger picture.

3. **Millennials (1981-1996):**

    - **What drives them:**
    They attach great importance to social and ecological impact.

    - **Leadership approach:**
    Show how their work has a positive impact on the community or the environment.

4. **4th generation Z (from 1997):**

    - **What drives them:**
    They expect purpose as standard and want to combine innovation and sustainability.

    - **Leadership approach:**
    Give them projects that address both technological and social challenges.

3) Purpose in various professional groups

1. **Technical professions:**

   - **Focus:**
   Concrete, measurable results and the solution of complex problems.

   - **Leadership approach:**
   Emphasize how their work promotes efficiency, precision and innovation, e.g. through shorter development times or technical excellence.

2. **Creative roles:**

   - **Focus:**
   Emotional impact and the opportunity to inspire others through their work.

   - **Management approach:**
   Focus on the impact of your work on customers, the brand or the corporate culture.

3. **HR and management staff:**

   - **Focus:**
   Development of people and long-term strategies.

   - **Leadership approach:**
   Show how their work creates the foundation for a strong corporate culture and ensures the overall success of the company.

4) Purpose as a bridge between generations

A strong purpose can connect generations by addressing shared values.

Strategies to promote purpose across generations:

1. **Collaborative projects:**
   Let teams from different generations work together to learn from each other and find common ground.

2. **Open communication:**
   Promote an exchange about the meaning of purpose in order to integrate different perspectives.

3. **Integration into the strategy:**
   Show how Purpose is linked to the company's long-term goals in order to appeal to all generations.

5) Purpose in hybrid teams

Hybrid teams need special approaches to make purpose tangible:

1. **Transparency:**

    - Communicate how each task - whether in the office or remotely - contributes to achieving common goals.

2. **Visibility:**

    - Use tools such as Miro or Microsoft Teams to make progress and contributions visible.

3. **Shared experiences:**

    - Organize hybrid team events that focus on the purpose, e.g. workshops on the company's vision.

6) Extreme ownership: taking responsibility for purpose

As described in *Extreme Ownership*, it is up to the manager to define the purpose, communicate it clearly and anchor it in the team.

Practical steps:

1. **Exemplify purpose:**
   Show through your behavior how important purpose is.

2. **Create clarity:**
   Communicate regularly how each individual's work contributes to the common purpose.

3. **Use feedback:**
   Get feedback to ensure that the purpose remains relevant and tangible for everyone.

7) Practical example: Purpose in my team

In my team, we used Purpose to strengthen collaboration between different generations and roles. Our vision of "actively shaping the next generation of a software platform with clear and intuitive interfaces" was complemented by Purpose: "Shorten development times, enable better collaboration and create sustainable software in the long term."

To realize this purpose, we have:

- **Collaborative workshops held:** Teams from different levels of experience worked together on concepts, which led to a better understanding and new ideas.

- **Organized regular updates:** We used tools such as TFS and Microsoft Teams to visualize progress and celebrate successes.

- **Feedback integrated:** Retrospectives helped to regularly reflect on the purpose and ensure that it remained relevant for everyone.

The result was a team that not only worked together more effectively, but was also more motivated because the purpose became tangible for everyone.

8) Conclusion: Purpose as a unifying element

Purpose is a powerful tool to unite and motivate multigenerational teams. Leaders who clearly define purpose and adapt it to the individual needs of their teams not only create a shared understanding, but also a culture of engagement and collaboration. In a hybrid and dynamic working world, purpose is the key to connecting generations and professional groups.

9) When purpose clashes: leadership with different values

The challenge: Differences between management and team

Values and purpose are key drivers of motivation and engagement - but what happens when management's priorities are not aligned with those of the team? This is not an uncommon situation, especially in organizations that are caught between short-term business goals and long-term social or environmental values.

A typical example: While management is focused on efficiency and financial results, the team strives for more meaning and long-term impact in its work. Such discrepancies can lead to frustration, loss of motivation and a break in team cohesion.

The role of the manager: building bridges

In such situations, it is up to the manager to act as a mediator between the two worlds. The trick is to respect both the goals of management and the needs of the team and to create common ground.

Strategies to harmonize differences in values

1. **Promote open communication:**
   - **Share the management perspective:** Explain to the team the background and constraints behind management decisions. Transparency creates understanding.
   - **Get the team's opinion:** Give the team the opportunity to express their concerns and ideas openly. Regular feedback rounds or moderated dialogs can help.
2. **Define a common purpose:**
   - Search for an overarching goal that unites both management and team.
   - Example: "Increasing efficiency through innovative and sustainable solutions" could combine both interests.
3. **Create space for team purpose:**
   - If the corporate purpose is not sufficient for the team, enable your own initiatives that create meaning, e.g. projects with a social or ecological impact.
   - Example: In addition to working on the core objectives, a team could also work on an internal sustainability project.

4. **Making success and progress visible:**
    - Regularly demonstrate how the team's work contributes to both the organization's goals and a larger purpose.
    - Celebrate small successes to maintain commitment.

10) Practical example: Strengthening purpose despite differences

In my team of PLC programmers, there was a moment when the management's requirement to focus on cost reduction met the team's desire for long-term technical excellence.

Solution:
- I initiated an open feedback session where the team could voice their concerns. At the same time, I explained the management's priorities and the constraints behind these decisions.
- Together, we developed a project that combined both objectives: we worked on a more efficient software platform that also enabled clearer interfaces and more sustainable processes.
- The team felt heard and motivated as we found a common vision that took both perspectives into account.

Result:

The project was not only successfully completed, but also strengthened the connection between the team and management, as both sides better understood each other's perspectives.

11) Conclusion: Using differences in values as an opportunity

A mismatch between the values of the management and those of the team does not necessarily have to be negative. With open communication, a clear mediating role and a willingness to define common goals, managers can turn such conflicts into opportunities. The key is to use purpose as a unifying element and to respect both individual and organizational values.

Chapter 9 Practical examples and lessons learned

Introduction: Learning through experience

Theory is important, but real insights come from practice. In this chapter, I share specific examples and experiences from my team that show how modern leadership can be successfully implemented. These examples highlight challenges, solutions and the valuable lessons I have learned from them.

1) Practical examples: Successful leadership in the modern working world

1. the transition to working from home: creating structure through agility

Challenge:

When the pandemic started, my team had to switch from an office-only model to working entirely from home. Many team members were concerned about the loss of structure and social interaction.

Solution approach:

- We introduced **daily stand-ups** to create clarity about priorities and tasks every morning.
- **Retrospectives** helped us to gather regular feedback and adapt our processes.
- Tools such as **Microsoft Teams** and **TFS** ensured transparency in projects and enabled seamless communication.

Result:

The team was able to remain productive and social cohesion was even strengthened by the regular meetings and retrospectives.

2. the introduction of hybrid working models: combining flexibility with structure

Challenge:

After returning to the office, it was clear that many team members wanted to retain the flexibility of working from home. At the same time, there was a risk that collaboration between office and remote employees would suffer.

Solution approach:

- We defined clear rules for hybrid models, e.g. fixed office days for team workshops and flexible home office days for concentrated work.
- Agile practices such as **dailies** and **Kanban boards** were retained to coordinate collaboration between remote and office employees.

Result:

The hybrid model allowed the team to take advantage of both worlds without compromising on productivity or team dynamics.

3. realize the vision of a new software platform

Challenge:

Our goal was to develop the next generation of a software platform with clear and intuitive interfaces. The complexity of the project placed high demands on collaboration between different teams and generations.

Solution approach:

- We developed a clear vision that emphasized both technical precision and cross-team collaboration: "Shorter development times, better collaboration, fewer dependencies and more sustainable software."

- Workshops helped to share this vision with all team members and define concrete milestones.

- Regular retrospectives and feedback sessions were used to review progress and remove obstacles.

Result:

The project was not only successfully implemented, but also led to improved cooperation and motivation within the team.

2) Lessons learned: Important insights for modern leadership

1. clarity and communication are crucial

Whether it's introducing new working models or implementing a vision, clear communication is key. Unclear expectations or goals lead to frustration and inefficient work.

Tip:

Communicate regularly, transparently and through various channels to ensure that all team members stay informed and engaged.

2. flexibility requires discipline

Flexibility is only effective if it is supported by clear structures. Agile methods such as sprints and dailies provide the framework in which flexibility and creativity can flourish.

Tip:

Use agile principles to create a balance between discipline and freedom.

3. purpose motivates when it is tangible

Purpose is only effective if employees recognize it in their daily work. Abstract visions must be translated into concrete goals that are linked to individual tasks.

Tip:
Regularly show how each individual's work contributes to the overall goal and celebrate successes to make the purpose visible.

4. generational diversity is a strength

Different perspectives and values in a multigenerational team can present challenges, but also offer enormous potential for innovation and collaboration.

Tip:

Encourage intergenerational exchange, e.g. through mentoring programs or collaborative projects that leverage the strengths of each generation.

5. technology as a supporter, not a substitute

Technological tools can facilitate processes and improve communication, but they cannot replace the interpersonal level of leadership.

Tip:

Use tools such as Microsoft Teams or Miro specifically to promote transparency and collaboration, but make sure not to neglect personal conversations and human contact.

3) Conclusion: Practice as the key to developing modern leadership

The practical examples and lessons learned in this chapter show that successful leadership is no coincidence. It requires clarity, adaptability and the conscious use of tools and methods that are tailored to the specific needs of the team. Modern leadership is a never-ending journey - and this is precisely where its strength lies.

Chapter 10 A look into the future

Introduction: Leadership in a changing world

The world of work is changing faster than ever before. Technologies such as artificial intelligence (AI), automation and digital platforms are driving innovation, while social values such as sustainability and diversity are becoming increasingly important. For managers, this means continuously adapting and developing long-term strategies at the same time.

This chapter takes a look at the trends that will shape the working world of tomorrow and offers approaches on how managers can respond to them.

1) Technological developments and their impact on leadership

Artificial intelligence (AI): opportunities and challenges

- **Opportunities:**
  AI can automate routine tasks, accelerate data analysis and create new opportunities for innovation. This allows managers to focus more on strategic tasks and team leadership.

- **Challenges:**
  The use of AI requires a deep understanding of the technology and the ability to address ethical issues such as data protection or job losses.

Practical approach:

- Integrate AI in a targeted manner to optimize processes without neglecting the human factor.

- Promote training so that employees can take advantage of AI.

Hybrid technologies for collaboration

- Virtual and augmented reality (VR/AR) could revolutionize hybrid collaboration by enabling immersive meetings or interactive workshops.

Practical approach:

- Experiment with new technologies to test their benefits for teamwork.
- Involve tech-savvy team members to develop innovative solutions.

2) Generational change and new expectations

Generation Alpha enters the world of work

- This generation will grow up with digital technologies and expects technology to be seamlessly integrated into everyday working life.
- At the same time, they value sustainability, social responsibility and flexibility.

Management approach:

- Develop a corporate culture that emphasizes innovation and values in equal measure.
- Promote an open feedback culture that supports the exchange between all generations.

The role of diversity and inclusion

- Teams are becoming increasingly diverse - in terms of age, cultural background and working styles.
- Managers must create an environment in which all voices are heard and diversity is used as a strength.

Management approach:

- Implement programs to promote inclusion, e.g. mentoring or intercultural training.
- Develop hybrid working models that are tailored to the needs of diverse teams.

3) Sustainability and social responsibility as management topics

Sustainability as the standard, not the exception

- Employees and customers expect companies to act sustainably - from their use of resources to the way they work.

Management approach:

- Communicate how sustainable practices are part of the corporate strategy.
- Involve the team to develop sustainable solutions, e.g. through workshops or innovation projects.

Social responsibility as a competitive advantage

- Companies that assume social responsibility attract committed employees and strengthen their brand.

Management approach:

- Support projects that have a positive social or ecological impact.

- Show your team how their work contributes directly to these initiatives.

4) Agility as the key to future viability

Agile leadership for dynamic markets

- The ability to adapt quickly to change is becoming the most important leadership quality.
- Agility means designing structures in such a way that they are flexible and yet stable enough for continuous adjustments.

Practical approach:

- Use agile methods such as sprints and retrospectives to promote flexibility.
- Create a culture of error that supports innovation and learning.

Purpose remains decisive

- Purpose will continue to be the key driver of employee engagement in the future. Managers must continuously adapt purpose and goals in order to remain relevant.

Practical approach:

- Regularly check whether the company vision is in line with employee expectations.
- Emphasize your team's contribution to long-term social and environmental goals.

5) Extreme ownership in the working world of tomorrow

The principles from *Extreme Ownership* will continue to be relevant in the future: Responsibility, adaptability and clear communication remain the basis of modern leadership.

Practical implementation:

1. **Take responsibility:**
   Remain flexible and take responsibility for actively utilizing new technologies and trends.

2. **Eliminate obstacles:**
   Identify potential challenges early on and develop solutions as a team.

3. **Live the vision:**
   Show through your behavior how important innovation, sustainability and collaboration are.

6) Practical example: Future-oriented leadership in my team

In my team of PLC programmers, we are already using approaches that prepare us for the future:

- **Technology integration:**
  We are experimenting with tools such as **Miro** for collaborative planning and automating repetitive tasks to create more time for innovation.

- **Agility and adaptability**
  : Through regular retrospectives and feedback rounds, we remain flexible and can react quickly to new requirements.

- **Sustainability and purpose:**
  Our vision of "actively shaping the next generation of a software platform with clear and intuitive interfaces" emphasizes not only efficiency, but also long-term collaboration between teams and the development of sustainable solutions.

The result is a team that is not only prepared to accept change, but actively helps to shape it.

7) Conclusion: leadership with a view to the future

The world of work will continue to be characterized by change and innovation. Managers who take responsibility, integrate technological and social trends and align their teams with a clear purpose will continue to be successful in the future. The future belongs to those who remain flexible, act courageously and are always willing to learn from experience.

Acknowledgments

No success is ever the work of a single person - and this book is no exception. I would like to thank everyone who has accompanied, supported and inspired me on my journey as a leader.

First of all, I would like to thank my team. You have not only been part of many of the experiences described here, but also the source of many lessons. Your commitment, your openness and your willingness to break new ground have made this journey possible.

Special thanks to my mentors and colleagues who have supported me with their knowledge and experience. Your advice and feedback have helped me to grow as a manager and to constantly adopt new perspectives.

I would also like to thank my family for having my back while I worked on this book. Your patience, understanding and support mean more to me than words can express.

Finally, I would like to thank all readers who are taking on the challenge of rethinking leadership in a changing world. It is you who will shape the working world of tomorrow.

I dedicate this book to you - the managers who courageously take responsibility and lead their team into the future with clarity, empathy and vision.

Bibliography

1) Primary literature

1. Willink, Jocko, and Leif Babin. *Extreme Ownership: How U.S. Navy SEALs Lead and Win.* St. Martin's Press, 2015.

2. Sutherland, Jeff. *Scrum: The Art of Doing Twice the Work in Half the Time.* Crown Business, 2014.

3. Goleman, Daniel. *Emotional Intelligence: Why It Can Matter More Than IQ.* Bantam, 1995.

4. Pink, Daniel H. *Drive: The Surprising Truth About What Motivates Us.* Riverhead Books, 2009.

5. Covey, Stephen R. *The 7 Habits of Highly Effective People.* Free Press, 1989.

2) Secondary literature

1. Collins, Jim. *Good to Great: Why Some Companies Make the Leap... and Others Don't.* Harper Business, 2001.

2. Laloux, Frederic. *Reinventing Organizations: A Guide to Creating Organizations Inspired by the Next Stage of Human Consciousness.* Nelson Parker, 2014.

3. Edmondson, Amy C. *The Fearless Organization: Creating Psychological Safety in the Workplace for Learning, Innovation, and Growth.* Wiley, 2018.

3) Online sources

1. Harvard Business Review. "The Case for Agility." Accessed on 01.12.2024, available at: www.hbr.org.
2. McKinsey & Company. "The Future of Work Post-COVID." Accessed on 01.12.2024, available at: www.mckinsey.com.

www.ingramcontent.com/pod-product-compliance
Lightning Source LLC
Chambersburg PA
CBHW071559220526
45469CB00003B/1062